# Reviews

It is my privilege and honor to have met and worked with such a successful professional, Sharon Farinholt. Sharon is an extremely effective leader with unmatched energy and enthusiasm. She is innovative, has a deep desire to learn new skills and is a successful entrepreneur and an outstanding colleague. Sharon also believes in making her community the best community it can be and devotes extensive time and energy to accomplish this goal.

— Dr. Cheryl Thompson-Stacy
President Emeritus
Laurel Ridge Community College

As one of Sharon Farinholt's cheerleaders, along her roads to success as an entrepreneur, I have witnessed her dedication, determination, and agility as a business owner and community servant.

The learned lessons shared in her new book, The Marathon of Running A Business, are vibrant reflections of business building weaved together with her personal passion as a runner.

Sharon shares keys to success like preparation, training, dedication, collaboration, continued development, creating key partnerships, and teamwork. What I especially love is the authenticity in her writing.

Take a run alongside her, especially if you are thinking of starting a business, or want to refresh yours. I am confident it will help keep you on course to your personal best.

— Cynthia Schneider
CEO
The Top of Virginia Regional Chamber

Having known Sharon the majority of my life has been a true privilege. Watching her grow in each phase of her life has been a lesson in both perseverance and determination. Sharon has never let anything stop her when it comes to getting what she wants. She became a successful entrepreneur by depending on her own passion to prevail. Failure has never been in her vocabulary. Her capacity to give to others and be their helping hand is why so many were there to cheer her onto her own victories. Whether it was one of her many marathons, or one of her business ventures, Sharon has always had her own personal cheering section rooting for her to make it to the finish line. She uses the same tools in business as she does in all other aspects of her life and that is how she created the successes she so greatly deserves.

— Ruth Ann Jewell
Life Long Friend

Looking for a quick read that will help you break through the fears and excuses that are holding you back from achieving your goals? Here it is. Sharon Farinholt has a talent for focusing on the most important steps to success, developing a strategic plan to achieve her goals and taking consistent action to make it happen. As a wife, mother of 7, marathon runner, business owner and entrepreneur, Sharon has discovered effective strategies for success in business and in life. She shares those strategies here.

— Suzette Neff, Broker ERA OakCrest Realty

An engaging and inspiring story that will motivate you to follow your dreams and help shatter the fear of taking risks."

— Jay W. Foreman, Best-selling author

# The Marathon of Running a Business

**Sharon Farinholt**

ISBN: 979-8-9872203-0-6
ISBN: 979-8-9872203-1-3 (eBook)

# Dedication

I dedicate this book to my husband, Matt, who always believes in me and encourages me in all my endeavors. Thank you for starting my morning with a hot cup of tea to motivate me each day.

I also dedicate this book to my 7 children in appreciation for all that they have sacrificed throughout the years and for supporting me throughout the many miles of life. Each of you inspire me to strive to be a better version of myself each day. Thank You Jake, Austin, Kelsea, Molly, Luke, Mary and Elena

Lastly, I dedicate this book to my beautiful grandchildren. I will forever be your cheerleader!

# Table of Contents

# Chapter 1
# The Truth

I have a confession to make. I am not a multi-millionaire. I have not made millions of dollars in business. And I have never won a marathon. For that matter, the only races I have ever won are a few small-town runs without many runners. My wins are the goals that I set for myself at each race and meeting or exceeding them.

If you are reading this book because you want to make millions, I hope this leads you toward your goal. If you are reading this book because you want to know what it takes to become an entrepreneur and to be successful, I hope that these words offer you encouragement and guidance along the way. Perhaps you are reading this to get a fresh start. Whatever the reason you pick up this book, my hope is that you find something in it that offers tools towards your success.

Success is measured differently for each and every one of us. Merriam-Webster Dictionary defines success as a *"favorable or desired outcome."* I may not ever be a multi-millionaire, but I am a successful entrepreneur who achieved a favorable or desired outcome. I look forward to more success in my life and am grateful for the success already achieved.

My success comes in the standards and goals I set for myself and in the rewards I receive in reaching them. I have strived for success in all areas of my life; however I have not always been successful in reaching these goals. I am easily disappointed when I don't attain a goal for which I have worked hard.

*A favorable and desired outcome* is something we should all be striving for in life and in business. Each day should be measured by this definition. The tools we put in place each and every day are our keys to success. The training plan we follow will guide us. It is in each one of us to be successful.

When I stand at the starting line of each race, I never know what lies ahead. Each race is different; each course is different. Do I stand there with the intent to win the race? Most of the time the answer to this is no. Before each race I consider the goal that I set for myself and what it will take to attain that goal. When I start to run, I'm committed. There is no turning back.

Starting a business is much the same. Start running, don't turn back. There have been many times over the years that I wanted to stop, to give up, to quit. Continuing to run is where you find success.

Injuries and setbacks can happen while training for a race. They take time and patience to heal. This is true of being in business. Somedays will be painful, others will have setbacks. Patience and resilience will be needed to continue to move forward.

Being in business is like running a marathon. I show up to the starting line well trained and prepared for the long run. I know it won't be easy, but the effort I put in will define the outcome. It is a challenge that I am ready to tackle.

My mindset must be in a good place right from the start. I know there are times during this race that I will have to stop those negative voices in my head. Just as in business, you must train your mind to be positive when your thoughts turn negative. When I'm physically exhausted, I must keep going.

The beginning of a race is always exciting. My adrenaline is pumping and my energy is high. I'm ready to take on the miles ahead of me with gusto even knowing it won't be easy.

The challenge to continue running comes when I start to tire, and the goal seems unachievable. This is mid-race, the up-hills and down-hills of the course add to my highs and my lows. The excitement is no longer there and I long to see the finish line. I keep running.

Towards the second half of the race, I hit the wall. I have to dig deep and push through. I want to quit. I don't care if I finish the run. I wish that I had never started. Each mile seems further apart than the last. My mind is in a bad place. I keep running.

As I'm heading towards the finish line with only a few miles to go, I start to feel better mentally and physically, even though I am tired. This is when I know I am getting close to achieving the goal I set for myself. The last few miles of a marathon are where I like to be in business. I see the rewards of my effort. It isn't easy getting here, but I know the journey is worth it. I keep running.

As I run toward the finish line, my pace picks up a bit. Somehow, I'm able to find a reserve that gives me the boost I need to get there. It is within my reach, I can see it now! Success is within my reach! I keep running...

The crowds, the music, the excitement...I cross the finish. I did it! I take in the moment and I smile enthusiastically. I take a deep breath and soak in the great feeling of achievement. I reflect on the many miles behind me and am so grateful to be standing where they have led me.

The road is long but oh so very exciting! Each step is one step closer to achieving a goal that I have set for myself. I have crossed many finish lines, and have owned several businesses. Each one has its own story. Each story I own.

There will be many marathons in business. The road will be filled with twists, turns, ups and downs. There will be many highs and many lows. All will be worth your efforts. Keep your head in the race, no regrets, leave it on the course. Success is within your reach. Now start running.

# Chapter 2
# The Journey

*I have worked hard for this…and now here I stand. My heart is pounding, my mind is racing, I am starting to second guess myself. Am I ready for this? Why did I think this was a good idea? I am going to be so tired! I do not have to do it. What if I can't finish the race? My adrenaline rushes, my mindset shifts. I have worked hard for this. I have trained many hours to reach this goal. I visualize the finish line in my mind. There are 26.2 miles between where I am standing now, and where I want to be. 26.2 miles…I can do this! No regrets, I've got this!*

Unless you have ever run a marathon, you may not know what goes on mentally at the starting line. You probably look at the runners and marvel at the fact that they are going to do something you may never try. If you have ever started a business…you know the exact feeling I have just described. Can I do this? It is going to be difficult. What if I fail? What if I FAIL? The starting gun fires, and I start running.

For years I would train and my goal at the start of a race, was to get to the finish line as quickly as possible. I would run past important landmarks, beautiful scenery, one foot in front of the other. The sound of the steady cadence of the pounding of my feet would be trance inducing. My mind would play games with me all along the way. My mind would tell me I can't, and my mindset would remind me that I can. When I would see the finish line I would give one last kick and cross the line. The adrenaline rush of finishing something I had worked so hard for is sure to be something like an addict feels with a "hit" of his drug of choice.

From start to finish, I had to continue to be focused, determined, persistent and consistent. The one piece I often missed, was enjoying the journey of the miles between the starting line and the finish line. As entrepreneurs, the same can be true. We can be so focused on the goal, that we forget to celebrate the wins in between.

When setting a goal, our mindset to reaching it is the first and probably most important step to reaching it. In today's world, there are so many distractions. We see shiny objects all day and forget to stay focused.

The journey in between is what keeps us going! Our training plan keeps us on track. A good training plan keeps you focused, and allows for a smoother journey along the way. I find when I put my training plan aside, I get off track. I am sloppy and my mindset gets out of whack.

On April 15th, 2013, I learned a valuable lesson. I had trained through rain, sleet, snow, and freezing temperatures to earn my spot at the start of the Boston Marathon. The Boston Marathon is one in which you have to qualify to be able to run. I had never qualified for this marathon before, so this was my first time to run this race. I decided that this would be the last marathon that I would ever run. Because I had decided this would be my last marathon, I wanted to experience it instead of racing to cross the finish line. I wanted to enjoy the journey of each mile in between from start to the end. Much like running a business, we need to enjoy the journey as we work towards our goal.

Putting together a training plan for a marathon can be a daunting task. However, once I put it together, look at it and visualize the plan, I can break it down. If I take it week by week, I will reach my goal. Sure, some days I may have to improvise, but I have a plan in place that will help guide me through the daily process of working towards 26.2 miles. In business, your training plan will guide you to successfully grow your business.

*I am at the starting line at The Boston Marathon. The loud sound of the starting cannon let all the runners know... the race has begun. There is no turning back now. Forward motion...I cannot quit. The weather is perfect, and I start to run. I take it all in, the sights along the way, the crowds cheering, the community handing out water and snacks as we wind the streets of Boston. The kids stand in line along the streets with outstretched hands wanting a high five as we run past them, and I smile as I smack their hands like a stack of dominoes as I run. It is not an easy run. I "hit the wall". It's only mile 17 (for runners this means your mind has to push you through when your body is telling you to stop) but I keep going. Only 9.2 miles left until I cross the finish line! I am tired, yet I am loving the journey along the way. I have planned well for this and I'm feeling great. I have been consistent in my training and that helps me push through the wall that my mind created. The only barrier is me and my mindset. I make no excuses; I can finish the race. I see the balloons in the distance and I can hear the crowds cheering as I'm getting closer. It's a beautiful sight, running down that last stretch to the finish. I am going to make it. I dig deep and pick up my speed, giving it my last effort to get there quickly so I can place the finisher medal around my neck that I have worked so hard to earn.*

My marathon story doesn't end well. I was only one minute and 46 seconds across the finish line when the terrorist bombs exploded at the finish of The Boston Marathon. I was in the finish chute when the heartbreaking chaos erupted. It was a moment in time I will never forget. I learned a valuable lesson that day…work hard to reach your goals, and remember to enjoy the journey along the way.

The sound and the feel of the explosion from the bomb that detonated as I ran across the finish line is something I will never forget. I was still in the finish chute, celebrating having reached my goal. And then the sound of the second explosion, rang in my ears. I turned back to look, and could only see a huge dark cloud of smoke. It was at that moment, that I realized we were being attacked. I had to make a decision. Do I fall and tremble in fear, or do I press on hoping for the best? Some of the runners who had just crossed the finish line with me started to run away, which nearly caused a stampede. I assessed the situation and quickly realized I was in survival mode…I may never see my family again. And I wasn't even sure that my husband had survived the explosions. He had been waiting for me at the finish line, I had no idea where he was now.

I had to dig deeper, and I had to make a plan. Yes, I was scared, but I didn't allow myself to break down and panic. The sirens blared, and for a moment, I stood wondering if I was in the middle of a movie scene, as it was all so surreal. My goal became to reunite with my husband, and get out of the city. The choice was mine; do I panic and break down or do I push the fear aside and work on a plan to survive? I took a deep breath, said a prayer, and moved forward toward survival.

Crossing the finish line of the Boston Marathon was one of the most exciting experiences I had accomplished. I remember the moment well when I crossed the line knowing that my months of training had paid off. When the terrorists' bombs changed celebration to terror, I knew I may not survive.

*Panic is all around me. Where is the next bomb planted? There is no place to hide, I keep moving forward as I try to formulate a plan. I just finished something I worked so hard for and I'm trying to wrap my head around what was happening. I look towards a table in the finish chute; there is a volunteer standing there who, just moments before, was smiling and placing medals around the neck of the finishers that had just crossed the line. She looks so scared. I walk over to the medal table and ask her if I can take one. I don't think she heard me, as she started to walk away to safety. I take a medal and place it around my neck. If I was going to die, I wanted to die with the medal on me.*

My memories of running the race that day are wonderful. Of all of the years of racing, this was my favorite race. No matter how painful each step was, embracing the steps toward the finish line made it more bearable and even enjoyable. The terrorist attack at the end of the race is something no one should ever have to go through or fear happening in their life. I will never forget that day, changing from celebration to survival. Those are the memories from which a bigger lesson was learned. Embrace each day as it comes. It's a gift that we can never get back. Embrace entrepreneurship the same way, it's scary, it's difficult, we don't know how it will end, but allow the highs and lows to guide you to your goal. Fear can steal you, or motivate you. In the end, the choice is yours.

*I have my name written in Sharpie down my arm during the Philadelphia Marathon. This allows spectators to cheer for me by name while I'm running. An anonymous spectator cheers my name, "No regrets, Sharon! Leave it on the course" she yells.*

The Philadelphia Marathon is the marathon where I qualified for The Boston Marathon by only 15 seconds. To be allowed to race in The Boston Marathon, you must earn a qualifying time upon completion of another marathon. Mile 21 I hit the wall during this marathon. This spectator must have seen the look on my face that let her know I was about to give up. I wanted to walk and my mind was telling me it was okay to do so. This lady who I will never know, encouraged me to keep going. "No regrets…leave it on the course." It's a mindset. This one sentence motivated me to keep moving towards my goal. And I qualified for the Boston Marathon because of it.

What motivates you to keep moving? How do you move forward from idea to goal? How often do you let fear paralyze you? How can you change your mindset to hit the ground running and to let obstacles be viewed as challenges instead of problems? What does your training plan look like?

You are at the starting line…the starting gun fires. You have a lot of miles ahead of you. You have trained hard and set goals. Your mind tells you; you cannot do this. Your mindset says "Go!" Don't forget to enjoy the miles in between, no matter how difficult they may be.

# Chapter 3
# Focus

*It's 4.30 in the morning and I have an important meeting later in the day. It is dark and cold outside. I've been training for weeks... the miles are getting longer. I have so much to do today. How can I possibly find time for a 19-mile-long run? Why did I think running a marathon was a good idea? No harm, no foul...I don't have to do this, I say to myself as I bundle up, grab my flashlight and quietly head out my front door to start my training run, careful not to wake the family as I close the door behind me.*

With every idea there comes a lot of other thoughts that can clutter your mind. Can I do this? What steps do I take? I can be rich! I'll be able to take trips! What if I lose everything? The list goes on. If you can stay focused, you can usually finish what you set out to do. The problem is the spiral in which we allow ourselves to be caught. Once we are in the spiral, it's tough to climb out. Once we do, we are tired and usually aren't sure where to begin. We have to re-focus on the original goal and decide if this is worth working hard and putting in the effort. Sometimes we must make a shift in our frame of mind that motivates us to pursue the goal we have been working towards.

The idea for a business is usually the easy step. Putting in the hard work and staying focused is the hard step. It's a mindset. It takes determination. "Excuses" is another name for failure. That may sound harsh, but for some reason making excuses is usually a lot easier than doing the work. If we don't do the work, we won't know success. Staying focused and having a positive mindset are keys to success. It isn't going to be easy. If you expect it to be, you may want to close shop before you ever open the doors. If you are up for the challenge, and tackle it as such, you may do okay. Don't let your mind fool you into thinking that being in business for oneself is going to be a walk in the park. It isn't. It's a marathon. You need to hit the ground running, look back to learn from mistakes, and use those mistakes to catapult you forward.

In 2008, I opened a retail recognition business. This was the start of the Great Recession. My husband and I had 7 children, and had put all of our savings into starting the business. I will never forget putting the first item on my display case in my showroom. It was a trophy, as trophies were a big part of what I sold. As I put the first trophy on the shelf I said out loud, "I have nowhere to go but up. Failure is not an option."

It was at that moment that I made a decision…failure is not an option. There is no plan B. I will do the work needed to succeed. The path won't be easy, but I am up for the challenge. Bring it on!

Many people would have let the start of a recession be an excuse for not continuing with the idea of opening a business. It was a risk I was willing to take. I knew I had to stay focused and work hard. I couldn't just open the doors of the business and expect the business to come to me. I had to go out and find the business and not make excuses. Making excuses for not following a plan can be the demise of a business. You must hit the ground running.

Starting a business is much like training for a race. You have to train to be a competitor. Being in business takes a trained mind. When I am training for a race, I plan out each week. How many miles will I run that week? How fast do I need to run to reach my goal? We should look at each week in business planning the same way. Your weekly business plan is your training log. It should be easy to plug in what needs to be completed each week to work towards your goal. Staying consistent is so important.

When I decided to open a business, my state of mind was set on accomplishing the goal of owning a successful business. I knew the road there would be filled with obstacles. I was afraid. I had everything to lose, and didn't know what I had to gain.

Fear and mindset go hand in hand. Fear can be what stops us from moving forward with any goal in life. For most of us, the fear of failure is bigger than the fear of what lies ahead. I didn't let that fear of the unknown stop me from pursuing my dream of being an entrepreneur. I allowed it to motivate me. Fear can paralyze or motivate. Mindset can paralyze or motivate. If you start by working on the mindset, you can overcome the fear. A well-trained mind can help turn the fear of failing into a plan for surviving.

We all know the children's book, The Little Engine that Could. That little engine used a mindset to make it up that hill. *"I think I can, I think I can, I know I can, I know I can."* And when he made it to the top, he celebrated his accomplishment.

The decision to move forward with opening my retail business came with focus, determination and a positive mindset. I had a great excuse not to open it, we were at the start of the Great Recession! I did a lot of research and felt that my community could support this business, if I was willing to put in the work. It doesn't happen for you! You must make a conscious effort every day to put one foot in front of the other and make it happen. It's a decision you make each day. Do I do the work that's needed to be successful? Or am I one of the many people who have a great idea, but don't do the carry-through needed for success?

What can you do to help you stay focused and to have a positive mindset? When I'm at the starting line of a race, I picture the finish line. I picture myself crossing the finish line. I don't think about the miles in between. I allow my mind to start the celebration, before the celebration begins. I know it's not going to be easy, but I have trained well for it and have stayed consistent with my training. The same is true in business.

What if you took baby steps with your business and found ways to celebrate the little wins? My dad used to always say to me, "Sharon, how do you eat an elephant? One bite at a time." I tend to want to bite off more than I can chew…in the moment. However, if I break my goals down into bite size pieces, I'm able to chew the elephant and enjoy the flavor along the way.

Set your goal, have a positive mindset, knowing that there are going to be obstacles along the way. Staying focused and doing the work that needs to be done is key to success. There are going to be curve balls thrown your way. Your legs are going to ache from "running" so long. You are going to be physically exhausted some days, and mentally exhausted others. You will "hit the wall."

Being in business is not for sissies. You must be willing to roll up your sleeves and put in the work. In most cases, the only one you have to blame for a lack of success is yourself. When you reach your goal, there is no blame. There is exhilaration. When you look back at what you have accomplished, pat yourself on the back grateful that you didn't give up, and you will start to move forward.

Setting goals is usually the easy part, reaching the goals takes mindset, discipline, and consistency. When you have the mindset of being the best at what you do, you are willing to put in the work to get there. Don't allow yourself to start thinking negative thoughts such as, "what will I do if this doesn't work?" "What's my plan B?" There is no plan B! Staying focused on your goal takes mental strength. Your goal: To be the best in my business. Your strategy: Work hard, stay consistent, and have a positive mindset. What's your training plan?

When I decide to run a race, I have to come up with a training plan. Running a marathon takes a 16-week training plan. Each week I break my plan into days. Each day, I figure out what I need to do to work towards my goal for the week. It's a strategy. The hard days are the days when I need to run a 15-mile training run in the middle of the week, and still get to work on time. It may be freezing cold outside, it might be pouring down rain, or even snowing. With determination and a positive mindset, I get it done.

What does your weekly business training log look like? What are the things you MUST accomplish because it's part of the business? (putting the orders together, working with customers, keeping up the books, etc.) Those are the things that you wake up each day knowing you must do. When I'm training for a race, I know I will need to do some kind of work-out each day when I wake. I don't have to write that down on my log. I do have to write down what the work-out looks like to work towards my goal.

What are the extras that you can add to your daily routine to be a better entrepreneur? These are the things that you will need to add to your business plan. To build a business, you must build your network. This will consist of the people who know you and are there to support you as you continue this journey as well as the people you have yet to meet that will help your business grow.

*I'm running through the streets of a city while running a marathon. The weather is perfect! I have my husband, Matt, strategically meeting me at the miles where I know I will struggle and I delight in the added stops he makes along the way to cheer me on. My mindset helps me get to the next mile. "I'm getting tired, I'm 10 miles in. Matt will be at mile marker 12! Yes! Onward to mile 12 where I know I will be greeted with a cheerful smile and words of encouragement!" I know I'm not alone. Matt is one of the key people in my network. The crowds cheer, they encourage me to continue moving.*

Who are your key people that are going to support you? You will want to quit. You can NOT do this alone. It may be your business, but you will need support to help you when you are physically and mentally exhausted. You need your people. Your weekly business plan had better have a few spaces for these key people. Yes, having time with your significant other, friends and family is key to the success of business. And if you don't make time for them, you had better count on this business journey being long and lonely.

*The crowds are cheering...they motivate me even though they do not know me. They have no idea who I am, yet they want me to succeed. I am surrounded by people who are smiling, laughing, holding a hand up to give me a high five. They are chanting words of encouragement, and they help my mindset stay focused on the goal...I will earn the medal for which I have worked and trained so hard. I will keep going.*

I am a big fan of networking events. For the most part, it's a group of people much like me...trying to grow a business. They give me their business card and tell me about the services they offer. I may know someone that needs their service, or perhaps I need their service. We plan to meet another day when we both can talk and share ideas on business growth. I always ask the question, "how can I help you grow your business" when I have these one-on-one meetings.

These are your fans. The people who want to help you grow are the ones on the sideline cheering you on! "You need a realtor? Sharon is a great one! Here is her business info." Your sideline cheerleaders are the key to your success! Are they part of your weekly training log? Do you have time put aside to attend networking events? Have you made time to get together after the event to get to know these people in your community better? These are also the people who can often help you think outside the box when you need a positive mindset reset. Let them in…don't think you can do this alone.

I have many great friends in my life, but only a handful that really want to help me be a better version of myself. These are the people I trust the most. Their honesty can drive me crazy at times, especially when I'm asking for advice. I want them to tell me what I want to hear. Instead they tell me what I need to hear. I try so very hard to convince them to think like me and to support my ideas. Although they are very supportive, they also know me well enough to know that some of my ideas may not be what is best for me. They help me see things in a different light. They don't shame or ridicule me. We all need our go-to people for encouragement and success.

When I owned my retail business, there were several times I wanted to quit. Failure was not an option, but was it okay to quit? Could I put a sign on the door that said, "Business is permanently closed" and not show up to run the business ever again? Was that acceptable? Money was tight, cash flow was not flowing, employees were hard to find and when you did find one you liked, they would often need to leave for school, military, or just to find something different to do. I was exhausted and I wanted to shut the doors for good. My mind was not in a good place.

It was these times that I needed support. Matt has always been my number one fan and has reminded me on more than one occasion that I'm not a quitter. My mom is my cheerleader. She has her pom-poms waving and lets me know how proud she is and that she is sure my dad is looking down from above with pride. My kids have also been there for me when things got rough. I remember my daughter saying to me, "Mom, you are the strongest woman I know. You will get through this!" And I did. When my mind said stop, my support helped me reset.

These were the times when I realized I had not stayed true to my "training plan." I hadn't found time to "breathe." I was suffocating in the "busyness" of business. My plan had not been touched in weeks. I missed my sideline cheerleaders. I needed to re-center and re-focus. I could not be successful without the success of others who have done this before me and are happy to help me grow.

I had a big trophy order due. A football league had called in a last-minute order of close to 300 trophies and about a dozen championship sized trophies. I did the math and realized that the number of minutes needed to complete this order were more than what I had. I reached out to a group of my friends and offered pizza and wine if they would be willing to come help me get this order completed. I will never forget being in my shop and seeing 7 of my closest friends standing around the production table, working, laughing and getting the order completed in time for delivery the next day. These were my cheerleaders, and I am grateful for them. Your cheerleaders are important. Make time for them! And remember to be there for them when needed, too.

Your training plan needs to be constantly evolving. Warning: this doesn't mean to keep changing direction. It means your plan evolves as you grow in business. Never be afraid to add new concepts to your plan. For instance, if you have "video content" as part of your weekly plan, find different ways to improve the content or different platforms to show your content.

When you are starting off, there will be much to learn. The most successful entrepreneurs learn how to work "on their business" while working in the business. A positive mindset and not being afraid to learn something new will do wonders. When I get too comfortable, I get stagnant. If I get stagnant, my business gets stagnant too. Don't make the mistake of getting too caught up in the busyness of business. Devise a plan to work ON your business more and IN your business less. You just may be surprised at how much growth will happen when you do this!

*I need to dig deep. I have put so many miles into this training. I do a mental check, my legs feel good, my breathing is not labored, my body temperature is not too hot or too cool, I have many miles to go. I can do this!*

# Chapter 4
# Mindset

*It is a beautiful morning for a run. My friend and I meet before my kids and husband have started to wake from their sleep. It is a typical morning at my house. I sneak out before the sun rises most mornings. It is my routine, and I am grateful for the accountability my friend offers that motivates me to do this each day. I look at my training log, today is a normal 6-mile run.*

When deciding on whether to start a new business venture, your training plan needs to begin before you open the doors of your business. Is your business something that is needed in your community? Can your community support it?

It always amazes me when I talk to others in business and ask them what homework they did BEFORE they opened their business only to find they have done little to prepare. This is a critical part of any training plan! A great idea, may not equal a great business. Are you doing a business as a hobby? Or do you have an entrepreneurial mindset and are you in business to make money? If it is to make money…you had better do your homework.

Before running a marathon, I talked to other distance runners. I asked them about the commitment it would take to complete a distance so long. They shared with me the difficulties of running a race that takes hours to complete and the challenge of the commitment leading up to the race. And every single one made it clear, that it is a mindset that will get me through.

These marathoners shared with me how difficult the training can be even when not running the miles. I will not be able to eat what everyone else is eating. I would need to sacrifice the cupcakes and fast food and eat healthy if I wanted to do well. While my friends may be having a late night get together, I will need to be at home getting rest in order to be ready for the long run the next day. There will be days of long exhausting runs, depleting me of energy needed to spend time enjoying family outings. I'll want to rest after running 18 miles.

"Why do you run these long races", I would ask. "Because it is a challenge, it keeps me focused and gives me a lofty goal to work towards. Each day when I attack the training plan head on and complete the training for the day, it gives me a great sense of accomplishment. I set a goal, and complete it."

There were other reasons as well, such as "I need to prove to myself that I can" or "I want to try to lose weight." But even those are met with the same challenges and mindset…I must do the work to reach the goal.

The same is true in business. When I decided to open my recognition business, I spent at least a month calling others in the same business. I asked them to share the good, the bad, the successes, and the learning moments. (I don't like to call those failures.)

I was not afraid to ask them their gross income. Each person I spoke to was very forthcoming with that information. I would ask them to share the first 3 years of sales income, because if your business makes it to 3 years, you should be able to succeed for many more.

To make people more comfortable sharing this information without concern of competition, I would call business owners in other states. In most cases, people want to help, if you only ask.

Therefore asking owners in other states that share the same demographics as mine was a good way to go…I wasn't a threat to their business.

Before beginning a career in Real Estate, I reached out to people who I knew were agents at one time as well as those who were currently agents. I listened to their stories of shifting markets, weekend showings, as well as the successes they had along the way.

Hearing the stories of others who had once been in the same business and those currently in the business of Real Estate was critical to my decision of whether or not to proceed. In Real Estate I spoke to other agents within my community to get a feel for what a week, a month, and a year looks like. Do not be afraid to ask… most people want to help.

Understanding what I was getting into was best learned by those who have traveled the same path before me. It helped me to decide whether I was up for all that was involved to make it a success. I also wanted to understand why those who closed the doors of the business did so. Educating oneself before starting a business is crucial.

I learned lessons about cash flow and having to have deep pockets to get started. In other words, if money is tight, I had better have a cash reserve to help pay the bills. Many people do not know this when starting a business. If part of your training plan is educating yourself by talking to those who have been in your line of business before you, you will not be quite as surprised when the "surprises" happen.

It is one thing to talk to others about their business, but seeing it in action can be a whole other ballgame. After many phone calls with people in the recognition business, I traveled to their retail location. Seeing a "day in the life" was amazing for me. For some it may have been enough to make you decide right there and then to not move forward. To me, it was a beautifully choreographed orchestra of many moving parts working together to create something beautiful for others to enjoy. Yes, it seemed hectic and busy. In fact, in each case the business owner would have to stop and answer phone calls, talk to a customer, or put out a fire. I stared in awe as I watched. THIS is the life of an entrepreneur. I want this life! I'm not afraid of this. Sidenote, I had never had a business class in my life! But I was all in…and decided to move forward.

When you watch the finishers at a race, they look tired, exhausted in fact. Some want to sit immediately, others even lie down. Sometimes they vomit right there at the finish line! But nearly every finisher accomplishes something big…they achieved the goal they set out to achieve. Although they are tired, they all share a sense of accomplishment. The arms fly up in the air in celebration, a huge smile crosses their face as they cross the line… they did it!

When I visited the businesses to get insight on what being an entrepreneur looks like, the people all looked much the same. When I looked in their eyes, I could see a spirit of success. I could see a passion that each one of them possessed. I could see a mindset that said, "I got this!" Even if they were struggling, I could see success. I wanted what they had.

The training plan needed before moving forward with a business plan should consist of time researching the business idea. Make sure you are comparing apples to apples. If you live in an area with a population of 150,000, don't meet with a business owner whose business is in a city of 400,000. The numbers are not going to be the same. When you do your homework, look at demographics.

If you have a great idea for the area you live in and no one else has done it before, there may be a reason for that. Make sure it is something your community can support. Be careful not to specialize in something that may not work well in your area. For instance, deciding to go into a business that only sells seashells in an area that is nowhere near the beach may not be a good idea. Certainly, you may have some sales. But most beach lovers tend to enjoy their shell searching while they are surfside. How many shells will you need to sell to pay rent, utilities, and vendors for inventory? Although you may love seashells, will there be enough seashell lovers to support this business and leave you with money left over to enjoy? Is it a business that is prime for growth? Maybe there is a reason "she sells seashells by the seashore!"

Enough about the pre-game training plan…let's jump into the training plan for business continued success!

*The air is crisp, and we are halfway through our morning run. "I want to run a marathon" I say, fully expecting my friend to talk me out of it. Her reply surprises me, "I'll help you train and will run it with you, if you will run a 50-miler with me the next month." I chuckle, surely, she is joking. She is serious. We made a commitment, she would help me train for my first marathon, and together we would run our first (and my only) 50-miler. We will come up with a training plan, set a goal, and accomplish it.*

# Chapter 5
# The Training Plan

*Mile 13.1, I'm halfway to the finish! I look at my arm where I have written in permanent marker the pace I want to be at each mile. I'm on goal, and I'm halfway there.*

When running a marathon, you are pounding pavement for 26.2 miles. That's a lot of time to get inside of your own head and to start considering reasons to quit. What keeps you going? How do you talk yourself into continuing to put one foot in front of the other?

There is a mile marker at each mile of a marathon. It lets you know how far you have gone, as well as how far you still need to go to reach your goal. I consider these mile markers my celebrations. They are my "wins." I made it to this mile, surely, I can make it to the next.

If I break the miles down into just that...miles...then 26.2 doesn't seem quite as daunting. Each mile is an opportunity to celebrate. You made it to another mile! You are one step closer to the goal. Although celebrating the mile marker wins of a marathon doesn't include a champagne toast at each mile, it does wonders for your mentality. YES, I did it! I smile big, raise a fist in achievement, and allow the rush of excitement to lead me to my next celebration…another mile marker.

In business, it's critical to celebrate your wins. It's so easy to experience burnout if you are continuing to run to the finish line without celebrating the wins. When working on your training plan, be sure to celebrate the wins you experience when completing the goals you set forth. Burnout comes when you just keep running and never stop to admire and celebrate the work you put in.

For example, your plan should have coffee dates with prospective customers/clients each week. Let's say you decide to set up 2 coffees a week every week for a month. When you look back at your training plan, did you achieve this? Then celebrate! It could be as simple as celebrating with treating yourself to a pedicure for your hard work and commitment.

As you get going and money starts coming in, make your goals bigger for the month. Did you make as much money as you set out to that month? These should be realistic goals that are written in your plan. Make your goals attainable, but not too easy.

As you are getting started in your business, it's important to have the tools set up for business success. Have you set up your Google my Business page? This gives your business a profile that people can go to where they will learn more about your business. This is where you should ask customers and clients to leave a review. You may also want to ask vendors to leave a review for you. This builds your credibility in your business.

Aside from having consistent weekly plans, you should also add time to learn something new. In other words, complete your normal weekly tasks that will help you to grow, but be sure to add something new to each month.

It is so important to stay consistent, but continue to add and tweak your plan as needed. As a realtor I have my weekly goals of 2 one-on-one coffees a week, 4 networking events a month, 10 touches each week (phone calls, texts, emails) and a few other weekly tasks. Added to my monthly plan, is "business growth" ideas.

Each month I take on the task of learning something new. It could be learning how to set up a Google my Business page and creating it. Or it may be something a bit more challenging such as learning how to do a podcast. This took a bit more time but I had my podcast up and running in a few weeks and have continued to air an episode twice a month since it's beginning.

Consistency is key! Business planning should be part of your weekly plan. I try to keep Fridays as my business planning day. I have several notebooks where I business brainstorm. Where do I want to be? How do I get there? It's amazing what carving out a few hours a week to dive deep into your business plan can do for you and your business.

I've mentioned a lot of key things to keep in mind when working on your training plan. Goals, consistency, persistence, celebrating, and routine. Write these down and keep them in front of you!

**Goals: Set weekly/monthly goals in business and life. Review these goals weekly. Celebrate the wins!**

**Consistent: Keep consistent in your plans. Follow your training plan each week.**

**Persistence: Don't give up. Even if you fall short one week, don't give up. If your sales drop one month, don't give up. If you have a business or family crisis, don't give up. Life is going to happen, adjust and continue with forward momentum.**

**Celebrate: Celebrate your wins! This keeps you going! It keeps you from suffering burnout.**

**Routine: None of the above will happen if you don't stick to a routine. My routine consists of waking early each morning,**

**running 4 miles, time for prayer/meditation, head into the office and start working on my training plan. What does your routine look like?**

Start with a week. What must you complete each week in the business? How much time are you putting into getting the work done ON your business? Each business requires a different training plan of sorts. Yet, they all still look somewhat the same.

Here is a quick breakdown of what my training plan looked like when I had a retail business and my current training plan in Real Estate. I think you will see some similarities.

**Retail Recognition Business:**

**Monday:**

9.00: Team meeting. Look at the week and what needs to be completed regarding orders.

10.00: Answer emails/phone calls. Place orders.

11.00: Reach out to past customers from same month the year before. Do they need another order this year?

12.00: Reach out to prospective clients. I call this data mining. Who else could benefit from my service? Pick up the phone and call or send an email or text. Look up organizations that may need my services. Ask friends to connect me to different businesses. Don't be salesy!

The rest of the afternoon consisted of completing any work that required more time in my business. Mornings were for working on my business.

**Tuesday:**

9.00: Stop by a business and drop off my business catalogs.

10.00: Send emails to prospective or past clients.

11.00: Grab coffee with a past or prospective client.

12.00: Work on social media.

**Wednesday:**

**Wednesday** would look a lot like **Monday**. I made sure I did my daily "touches" of calls and emails.

**Thursday:**

**Thursday** looked a lot like **Tuesday**. I set **Tuesdays** and **Thursdays** aside for coffees.

**Friday:**

Business planning day! Review the week. What worked well. What is something new I can add to better my business? Learn something new and work on implementing it.

Each week I also made time for at least one networking event. These events gave me the contacts and connections to set up coffee dates and were added to my database.

**Real Estate:**

**Monday:**

9.00: Team meeting. Look at what's coming ahead and what's been completed.

10.00: Reach out to past clients and prospective clients using my sphere of influence. Check in on past clients and prospective clients, see if they want to be added to neighborhood news.

11.00: Send cards, notes and well wishes to prospective/past clients. Look at social media to see who may deserve some recognition.

12.00: Spend time on social media responding to posts building the relationships.

**Tuesday:**

9.00: Coffee Dates.

10.00: Work on social media content. Set up social media planner.

11.00: Work on mailings and newsletter content.

1.00: Record podcast.

**Wednesday and Thursday pretty much mirror Monday and Tuesday.**

**Friday** is my business planning day as well as my podcast editing day. I use this day to work on my business and to see what is working and what may need improving. I also use **Fridays** to learn something new. This could be as simple as learning a new social media platform or how to use a CRM (Customer Relationship Manager) program to better benefit my business.

As you can see, this plan should work with just about any small business. It is easy enough to tweak. This is what has worked for me in my two industries. Depending on your business industry, yours may look different. The important thing is to develop a weekly plan and work the plan, every week. Consistency is key. The main thing is to get into a routine and stay consistent. Don't let set-backs bring you down, they will happen. Work on your goals and celebrate the wins. Growth will start happening. Do Not Give Up! There is NO Plan B! Be Relentless!

BUSINESS TRAINING PLAN

| | Monday | Tuesday | Wednesday | Thursday | Friday |
|---|---|---|---|---|---|
| 08:00 | exercise/prayer | exercise/pray | exercise/pray | exercise/pray | exercise/pray |
| 09:00 | Review work week tasks | Coffee Dates | Morning networking | Coffee Dates | Business Planning |
| 10:00 | Contact current clients | Social Media | Notes, Cards for clients | Social Media | Business Planning |
| 11:00 | Data Mining: perspective clients | Mailings Newsletter | Data Mining: perspective clients | Event Planning | Business Planning |
| 12:00 | Lunch | Lunch | Lunch | Lunch | Lunch |
| 1:00 | Social Media | Record Podcast | Edit Podcast | Work on Video Content | catch up |
| 2:00 | work in business | work in business | work in business | Record Podcast | catch up |
| 3:00 | work in business | work in business | work in business | Work in business | Finish Early |

Make time for evening network events

*It is pouring rain and is quite chilly for my first marathon. The year is 1994 and my friend and I are running The Marine Corps Marathon in Washington, DC. I have two goals: 1. Finish under 4.00 hours. 2. Talk to Oprah Winfrey along the way. I know Oprah is ahead of me, because of her celebrity status, she is able to start the race before the rest of the runners. I search the crowd of runners as I make my way towards the finish. There's Oprah ahead! I catch up and introduce myself to her as I'm running alongside her. I tell her it is also my first marathon and we wish each other luck. My friend shakes her head in disbelief, then we head toward the finish line. I finish just under 4 hours, and I talked to Oprah. Goals Accomplished!*

# Chapter 6
# Challenge of Change

*My heart is beating, but I am numb and I can't feel a thing. My ears are ringing, there is activity going on around me, but I'm not present. I find a chair and I sit. An employee comes up to me and asks if I'm okay and I quickly snap back into reality, put a smile on my face and answer with an attempt at a cheerful, "Yes, I'm fine." I know she sees through me. She walks away, and gives me the space I need to regroup.*

My husband had called me a few minutes before this. He let me know he was laid off work. He would receive one month of severance pay. Most of our savings went toward opening my retail business. I was two years into the business, and had just reached my break-even point. We were using his paycheck to live on and I had only just started cutting a paycheck for myself, and it was minimal. It certainly was not enough to support a family of 7.

*I step outside hoping the fresh air will snap me out of this bad dream. I don't want to see or talk to anyone. I want to run. This run would not be training for a race. Nor would it be a casual daily run. I want to run away from the nightmare playing out in front of me. I want to run until I can run no longer. I want to run away from my problems.*

*Life is happening around me. I smile to one of my customers as I walk outside the door of my business hoping that my employee does not call me back in for assistance. The cool air feels good on my face as I start to walk. My thoughts are swirling as I contemplate my next steps.*

What started off as a normal day, changed in an instant. A typical day in business usually has some challenges. I like to call these normal daily challenges "fires to put out." This was not a normal fire. It was a three-alarm fire. It was going to take a lot more effort to extinguish. The answer to solving the problem was not right in front of me. It would take some time and patience to solve.

Failure was not an option. There was no plan B, only a plan A…be successful. There was not a place in my training plan where I had carved out, "what to do when you are about to run out of money." I was scared, and I allowed myself that night to marinade on what had happened. Closing the business was absolutely not an option, too much had gone into it at that point, financially, physically and emotionally.

A new strategy was needed for success. I could have continued with business as normal and hoped for the best; no changes to my game plan would be the worst thing I could do for my business. I had bills to pay, employees to pay, orders to fill, I had to make some changes. It would have been easy to stay in my comfort zone. My comfort zone made me feel in control, when my world was spiraling out of control. In my comfort zone I felt safe, when in reality, I was afraid. I had to step outside my comfort zone to survive.

What was my strategy for survival? There were many things about my training plan that needed to stay the same. I had to continue marketing my business, however, I now had to bump that up to another level. I spent evenings sending emails to prospective clients, after working all day. I reached out to everyone and anyone that I thought could possibly help me get business. I was not afraid to ask my friends to help spread the word and to connect me to friends of theirs who may benefit from my what my business offered.

My training plan now included a strategy on how to cut costs. What subscriptions could I cancel? What services could I do without? Had I even taken the time to compare vendor pricing? Up to that point, I had not. That became part of my plan. I created spreadsheets of my main vendors and listed the items ordered the most and the costs from each vendor. This allowed me to see which vendor to use to keep more money in the business, and which vendors to use only when needed.

Being pro-active gave me the drive to keep moving forward! I've hit a wall, how do I move past it? I was determined to find a way and found myself looking forward to the evenings when I could bury myself into business growth. At the end of each day, I could look back and see everything I had accomplished. I didn't allow the setback to paralyze me. I used it to catapult my business to another level.

My husband's job loss helped me find ways to make my business stronger. As a marathoner, you have to strengthen all of your muscles, not just your legs. Your whole body needs to be strong to reach the finish line, including your brain. Being an entrepreneur is much the same! Keeping your business healthy and fit leads to success. Keeping your mind healthy and positive is critical. His job loss helped my business succeed. I celebrated what I had learned in that process and how applying it made for a healthier mindset and business. The journey was not easy…there were some hurdles to jump. When faced with a hurdle you are faced with two choices, stop, or dig deep and jump! If you choose to stop, the choice has been made for you. Get your best stride going, put your head in the game, stay focused, and jump!

Putting these new habits in place became part of my training plan. I kept up my robust marketing and kept a close eye on my expenses moving forward. Your training plan must stay consistent, but must always be evolving. Your journey will always have new adventures and surprises along the way! Embrace the journey and allow the experiences to help you grow.

That year in business was not easy. I broke my plan into bite sized pieces. Each month I could see the hard work paying off. I celebrated the wins and learned from any losses. I worked hard, and relished in the rewards of my hard work. That year my business grew and I continued to use these new habits moving forward. To this day you can still find me sitting in my recliner in the evening, watching my favorite show, and working on marketing or other business growth. My Real Estate business has benefited from this habit, and I am grateful.

Believe in yourself. There is so much packed into these three words. Others may believe in you, but if you don't believe in yourself what others think really doesn't matter. Remember that little engine? *"I think I can, I know I can!"* Each day you awaken you are given the gift of another day! How wonderful is that? Make a conscious effort every morning to remind yourself that you can and you will do whatever it takes to be successful. Don't let negativity get in the way of your positivity. Every day is a chance to start fresh!

Challenges are going to stop us in our tracks or make us want to run. Some challenges will be more difficult than others to overcome. Don't give up. Persevere.

*My heart is beating, but I am numb and I can't feel a thing. My ears are ringing, there is activity going on around me, it's all surreal. I just finished running the Boston Marathon where I felt the ground shake beneath me from two bombs. I'm in survival mode. I will survive. I will do whatever I can to keep moving forward. I am "Boston Strong."*

The truth is, when faced with a do or die situation in life or business, we can all choose to be Boston Strong. Stay focused and determined. You will survive.

# Chapter 7
# Miles of Success

*The adrenaline rush is huge…it is what keeps me going. The excitement of accomplishing something so unimaginable motivates me. The many miles towards entrepreneurship are exhilarating. I can do this…and I will. I am full of optimism.*

Mile one is usually the easiest mile. Mile one I am still smiling. I'm adjusting my pace and am taking in everyone and everything around me. I'm not too hot, not too chilly, I'm not thirsty, my body doesn't ache. My endorphins have kicked in, and I'm experiencing the "runner's high." It's a great feeling. I feel like I can run for miles. I know there is nothing stopping me! My determination will lead to victory. There is no questioning that. Nothing will stop me from continuing the miles that are between mile one and mile 26.2!

And then I hit mile 10, mile 12, mile 17 and it is not easy. My body says go; my mind says stop. Everything is hurting by mile 20 and the journey isn't what I thought it was going to be when I started at mile one.

Where did my endorphins go? My runner's high is no longer, it's just me and the pavement. That long stretch of pavement seems never ending. I am tired, and I am running out of steam.

I'm running out of endurance, and this no longer seems fun. There are orders due, employees have quit, and the hours at the office are long. The reality of being a business owner has hit me hard. I'm ready to call it quits. I have hit the wall.

Who am I? I am not a quitter. I've had some set-backs, but I am not a quitter. I have some aching muscles that could use a little massaging, but I won't quit. I have found myself down in the valley, I'm no longer standing tall on the mountain.

I have two choices here…stay in the valley, or start climbing up that mountain. As a runner, I have trained for the hills. I will go slowly, and allow my breathing to steady me as I run to the top. Hills allow me to re-focus. Don't look up. The mountain looks too high and if I allow my mind to play games with me, the mountain will look almost impossible to conquer. Don't look up. Look straight ahead. Forge the path with the tenacity and relentless effort that will allow you to reach the top.

The easier thing would have been not to allow myself to fall in the valley. But the truth is, it will happen. I don't know a business owner yet that hasn't stumbled downhill at some point. Let's face it, the downhills are much easier than climbing up. When we allow ourselves to stride along with no cares in the world, we find we have enjoyed the downhill ride so much, that we forgot to work to stay on top.

*The road is flat, there are no crowds cheering me. I'm holding steady and it feels pretty easy. I'm striding along, feeling good. Then I look at my watch. My times have slowed. How will I hit my goal? I got too comfortable, What do I need to do to make up time? I pick up my pace, I get my head back in the game and I re-focus.*

Five years into my retail business, I was feeling pretty good. I was comfortable. It had been smooth sailing that year. Then, I looked at my sales from the previous year and compared them. My sales were flat. My comfort led to no growth. We only grow when we feel uncomfortable.

I had to make a decision. With sales flat, and costs up, I had actually lost money. I needed to adjust my plan and I had to find a way to get out of my comfort zone. What I had in place worked to keep me in business for the time being, but would not continue to work if I wanted to be successful and grow in business.

Remember earlier when I mentioned calling others who were in the same line of business as you? I built relationships with some of those people and had stayed in touch with them. I reached out to one business owner who had really mentored me and he gave me the advice I already knew, but I needed to hear again. I had to think outside the box.

What need was missing in our community that I could fill through my business? As an entrepreneur you are a problem solver. My problem was I needed to find a way to bring in more money. The solution, I became the recognition specialist in our community that specialized in donor walls, naming walls, and I worked closely with the non-profits to build the reputation of being the go-to place for these items.

I needed to put a plan in place to make this happen. It would be a risk to take, as I had never taken on something this big in my 5 years of business. But it would be a calculated risk. I would learn everything I needed to know about specializing in these big donor walls that one sees in hospitals and other non-profit buildings. I needed to understand the process and know that I could do it and do it well.

I traveled to a sign manufacturing facility in North Carolina where I watched the production. I learned how donor walls were made and how to install them. I met with several vendors and discussed options. And in a few months' time, I became known as the donor wall specialist in our area and my sales soared.

There would be many other walls I would hit over the next few years in business. Employees would leave, I would lose a big account, cash flow would be tight, to name a few. Each time I would have to figure out how to push through the wall to get to the other side. Often the wall felt like it was made out of bricks and I would wonder if I would ever find the energy, mentally or physically, to get to the other side. I would dig deep to find the reserve that I needed to give me the strength to keep pushing through. These moments in business are tough, but the lessons learned through them can be invaluable.

Looking back at the years in business at my recognition shop I can see the progress that was made through every hurdle that seemed impossible. I learned how perseverance and determination got me through many obstacles. Never give up! Personal and business growth is earned through every challenge accepted.

I loved my years in business as a recognition specialist. It gave me great joy to see the awards and recognition walls I had created hanging in businesses throughout my town. Seeing pictures on social media with a winning team holding the coveted custom golden cup that I had helped design made my day! The work was not easy, but was well worth it.

After 11 years of being in this business, I decided it was time for a change. My family circumstances had changed from when I started the business. Our youngest, who used to play in the playroom after pre-school, was getting ready to graduate from high school. We now had grandchildren and I wanted to be able to spend more time with them. It was with a heavy heart, that I made the decision to sell. It wasn't an easy decision…this was my baby. It would be difficult leaving a business that had become part of who I was for 11 years.

Who am I? I know who I am not, I am not one that gives up easily. I am not one that stops when the going gets tough. I am not one that throws in the towel. My mindset is steadfast on accomplishing the goal, and I know I may have to dig deep to get there.

What motivates me? Hitting the wall motivates me. Stumbling to the valley motivates me. Knowing I have hills to conquer motivates me. Working on being the very best at what I do, motivates me. Hard work motivates me. Fear motivates me. My dad used to say to me, "Sharon, you need to roll the dice! Take a chance in life! Don't be afraid to take a chance." Much like my father, taking chances motivates me.

I remember well, sitting at my retail shop as I was getting ready to sell it. My employees had said their goodbyes and left to go home. It was just me and my business there. I slowly walked in each room and looked at what I had created! There were times I wanted to quit. I would be lying if I said I didn't shed some tears along the way. I stopped, and I took it all in. I soaked in all of it for probably an hour. It was so peaceful. You know that feeling when you dive under water and all of the noise around you disappears for a moment? It was like that…I soaked up all that I had created in 11 years before selling it. I soaked up every bit of it, all that I had learned, all that I been through. And I was damn proud. My heart and soul went into this business. She was my baby that I had raised, and much like parenting, I never gave up. I walked out the door one last time, looked back and shut off the light. I am an entrepreneur and the spirit of business is in me. I will take the spirit forward as I venture onto the next business.

Who am I? I am an entrepreneur, I am a marathoner, I am a wife, I am a mother, I am someone who doesn't give up in the face of adversity. Who are you? What keeps you going? What motivates you? What risks are you willing to take?

The journey is long, but can be so very rewarding. Remember to look back at your journey regularly. Where you were, where you are now. Who you were, who you are now. The journey is part of you now, it has formed you, and if you have traveled the path well, you just may be a better person because of it! You are an entrepreneur and innovation is what motivates you. Prepare for the road ahead and you will do great things!

*I look back, the miles have been long. I've trained hard. It hasn't been easy. I fell a few times, but I always got back up. It's been a good run, and I have learned so much and have met so many people who have inspired me along the way. Tomorrow, I hand the keys over to the new owner. I think back to The Boston Marathon, the moment when I hung that medal around my own neck to celebrate accomplishing something for which I had worked so hard. Isn't it ironic, I own a business where I make custom medals, yet I don't have a medal to place around my neck this evening to celebrate accomplishing the goal of being a successful business owner? I take a deep breath, turn out the lights of my retail business one last time. I close my eyes, smile and I celebrate.*

# Chapter 8
# Failure; Not an Option

*The cool salty air from the ocean breeze feels good on my skin. I am heading to the finish line of a half marathon. I can hear the music and can feel the energy as I get closer to the finish. I see the balloons, the people cheering, and I start to cry as I cross the finish line. I lean over as my knees buckle. A volunteer helps me, and places the finish medal around my neck and asks "are you okay?" I hug her and answer between tears, "this is the first race I have finished since being in the Boston bombing." She hugs me tighter. I am grateful for her. I hold my medal, and head out of the finish chute.*

You never really know how you will feel when you cross a finish line until you cross it. I have cheered, celebrated and even cried when coming to that point in a race. The emotions can be varied when completing something I have trained so hard to complete. The finish line is why you even begin the journey. You can't enjoy the celebration of the finish line if you never cross the starting line.

Some finish lines are more difficult than others to reach for many different reasons. When I crossed the finish line of the Richmond Marathon I dropped to my knees and wept. I ran that race in memory of my dad who had passed away months before race day. When

I reached the finish line of the one and only 50-miler I had run, I wept with sheer exhaustion from running for so many hours. Each finish line is an accomplishment, even if I don't always run a perfect race or get the finishing time, I had set out to achieve. I still finished the race, and that's always worth celebrating.

In the marathon of business, you will cross many finish lines. I always like to look at the end of each year as a finish line I'm working towards. Did I meet my goals? Did I do better this year than last? Did I find ways to improve my business? I allow myself to review the past year and to take in the celebration of my achievements of that year.

There are finish lines you will sprint to, and other finish lines that will feel more like running a marathon. Goal setting, discipline, focus, determination, and a good training plan will help you cross many finish lines. Sometimes you may crawl to the line, barely making it. Other times, you will cross the finish line and be so busy that you forget to stop to catch your breath before moving on to the next.

Getting to the finish line in a race can be painful. Reaching a business finish line can hurt, too. There are blisters on your feet, yet you keep going. Each step is painful, but each step is closer to your goal. Your determination helps you work through the growing pains, knowing your reward at the end will be well worth the effort you have put in.

When working on your training plan, your finish lines are the rewards for your efforts. When you get a business account you have been working hard to get, you crossed a finish line! When you have put the time in to learn a new software program that saves your business money, you crossed another finish line. Take it all in...you have worked hard for this!

That last day at my retail shop, I crossed a big finish line. If it were a scene in a movie, there would have been a replay of 11 years of cheers and tears in a few minutes clip playing in my head.

I closed my eyes and smiled. There were many times in those 11 years where I had fallen to my knees and struggled to get back up. Those were the times when I found a friendly hand reaching out to help me get back on my feet. There were times when personal struggles in my life were happening that made it difficult to even want to get out of bed, much less work towards a business goal. Many times, the finish line seemed out of reach. And other times, the journey to the finish was filled with great accomplishments and the rewards made it all worth it!

There were no cheers, there was no finish clock that read 96426 hours, which is still less than the number of hours I put in if you counted the research I did beforehand. It didn't matter! I knew what I had accomplished…and I celebrated.

Now, I was on to my next journey, a new race, a new finish line to cross, my new career. January 1st, 2020 was my last day at my retail business. March 1st 2020 was my first day as a licensed REALTOR®. I completed the Real Estate course, passed the state and national exam, and was ready to start my next business venture.

With great enthusiasm and energy, I was ready to take on this new venture with the same motto as my previous business…failure was not an option, there is no plan B. It was time to move onto something new. Using the skills, I had learned from the past, I started to work in the present, to create a successful future. It was a challenge I was ready to face head on.

This new career gave me the opportunity to continue doing what I love…helping other people. The tools I had learned in my previous career helped set me up for success in this new career. There was a lot to learn and I was excited to start something new. My classes were complete, I had passed my exam, I was at the starting line and ready to go!

The starting gun fired…and I was off and running the first day of March. Then something I never could have expected or predicted happened. A pandemic plagued our world and by April I was one of the earliest in our community to contract COVID 19. This wasn't part of the training plan. The world shut down. The race came to a screeching halt. Because not much was known about the virus at the time, people didn't want to be around me for a while for fear that I may still be carrying the virus even two months later. How do you move forward when it's hard to even know if a finish line exists? How do you keep the momentum? My training plan looked empty. I didn't know how to fill my plan and what direction to go to grow. The agency where I began as an agent had nearly shut down. Training was minimal and I struggled to gain momentum when I was pretty much racing alone.

It was a tough time for so many business owners. Everyone was being told to find a way to pivot in their business and I was left wondering how to "pivot" in a business that hadn't really even begun. I started to second guess continuing in Real Estate. It's not really failing if I never really start the business, is it?

Only, I had begun. I had worked hard for months to get through the Real Estate class. I had studied for months to pass both exams. I had passed the exams and I was a licensed REALTOR®. I had started the race, I had set my pace, I was comfortable getting the business started, and now I felt very uncomfortable. Do I back out of the race? Do I quit, or do I dig deep and keep running to the next finish line? There is no Plan B, only a Plan A; start my career in Real Estate. It's not going to be easy, but that's how I know I am growing. Change is never easy, that's part of the challenge. Business is challenging, the rewards are worth facing the challenge.

*I want to celebrate, but I can't stop feeling so emotional. I should be smiling and raising my hands up in celebration for completing a Half Marathon. I wipe the tears from my eyes. I did it. I faced a fear head on. There were crowds and there was chaos, but it was good chaos. This race hadn't ended in tragedy, as the Boston Marathon had when I crossed the finish line. I look out at the ocean and I breathe in the fresh air. I didn't let the fear of the unknown stop me from starting. I ran that race in honor and memory of everyone who had been injured or lost their life during the horror of the Boston Bombing.*

# Chapter 9
# Adventure of Uncertainty

*The course is flat, and it's supposedly a fast course. My goal: to qualify for the Boston Marathon one more time. I want to go back, and not allow fear to stop me. I want to re-live the excitement of the race; with a happy ending. I'm running through the wooded trail and it's strangely quiet for a marathon. It's a smaller race, and there are many miles with no spectators cheering.*

The struggle is real, how do I market a business of which I know so very little? I'm frustrated. I'm alone, which in turn, means I'm lonely. I have to navigate the path alone. There are only a few races where I found myself on the course with no one else around me and I wondered if I was making the correct turn. Was I still on course? I felt much like this at this point of my Real Estate career.

Which direction do I go when there are no course marshals directing me to "turn left", "turn right," "watch the potholes", and "right around the corner there is water ahead." The water table in a race was my lifeline. It's where I could re-hydrate, re-focus, and re-energize. When starting my Real Estate career during a pandemic, I couldn't find the water table. I was running with no direction. I was thirsty, but was struggling to find a way to quench the thirst.

To be fair, many people in business were lost at this time. None of us had ever lived through a pandemic. It was a difficult time. As my mind wrestled with whether to move forward with my plan of being a REALTOR®, my heart knew it was what I wanted to do. What was causing my resistance? Why was I feeling stuck?

I had hit the wall, and I was reminded of that moment during the Great Recession where I put the first trophy on my showroom shelf and said out loud, "failure is not an option." I had survived the Great Recession, I am Boston Strong, I can do this if I really get my head in the game and figure out a new strategy. I will not quit, my Plan A needed to be tweaked. I can and will move forward. I found my "water table", my mindset, and re-hydrated, re-focused, and re-energized. My training plan was empty; that would get me nowhere. I had to figure out what my new plan looked like. Meeting people face to face was barely an option due to the health concerns of COVID 19 in our country.

The office where I worked was pretty much empty. Zoom had become the new meeting platform, and even those were few and far between. I am a relational person, and I needed to be at a place where I could work with others who would mentor me and help me grow. I needed to find a place to call "home" where I could learn and grow through collaboration. I had to find a way to continue moving forward in my career, instead of struggling to find reasons to quit. Failure was not an option.

Six months after being licensed in Real Estate, I moved to another agency where I was given the tools I needed to help boost my confidence and to grow. I found mentors who would answer my questions and offer guidance and I soaked in everything I could. My empty training plan was ready to be filled with new ways to move forward and to grow. I was on course, and this move helped me gain momentum and reach the finish line of my first year. My goal as I began my business in 2020 was 3 closings by the end of my first year. By the end of December, I had 7 closings!

The beginning of 2020 I began my new business, a pandemic hit, our country shut down, and when my mind told me to quit, my mindset said to keep going. It frustrates me when people tell me I was lucky to get into Real Estate when I did. They mean well, but it insinuates that I didn't have to work hard to reach my goals.

There are many great Real Estate agents in my community that have been doing this for years. I had to work hard to find my place and to build my business. It wasn't handed to me. I learned from these other agents and appreciated what each one taught me during every transaction and closing. I asked a lot of questions to agents in my agency and found that they were happy to help me learn. I surrounded myself with people who wanted to help me with my success, even though I was a competitor. I collaborated and grew. I filled in my training plan with a daily to-do list and followed it. I set weekly goals to encourage growth, and my business grew.

Overall, my training plan didn't look too different from the plan I used with my previous business. Meeting people in person to network wasn't as easy during COVID 19, so I filled my plan with Zoom meetings and phone calls. I reached out to friends each week and when I was able to meet in person to hand them a stack of my business cards to share with others, I would do so. If meeting in person didn't work, I called and asked if I could mail a stack of my business cards to them. I set a goal each week to reach out directly to 30 contacts and broke that into 5 days. Yes, COVID caused some challenges but I found a way to work around the challenges so that I was able to keep networking and building relationships.

My training plan allows for time for learning new things and business development. Although in-person training had been put on hold during the pandemic, I found that YouTube and other platforms such as Zoom had much to offer in continued education. This allowed me to continue to grow in my knowledge of Real Estate and business. During this time, I took an online class to learn how to start a podcast and now the podcast has become part of my weekly training plan.

This was a challenging time for small businesses and most people wouldn't have even considered starting a business during the pandemic. My business started weeks before the pandemic hit, it would have been a perfect reason to not move forward with it. Excuses are a great way to stop progress, execution is the best way to perfect progress. It's a choice every entrepreneur has to make many times during their career, and if they choose execution each time the progress made will be well worth it.

The pandemic had stopped everyone in their tracks. What am I training for? Why should I keep running? There are no marathons, there are no 5K's. Why should I step outside and put one foot in front of the other that leads to that steady rhythm of a run if there is nothing to train for?

*I'm running down my country roads in silence. There is not much activity going on in my small little town. I breathe hard, the Coronavirus has made my lungs work harder than they used to need to work during a run. Each deep breath takes more effort as I am recovering from COVID. Slowly I continue my run. It's my routine, it's what I have done for years. It just feels right. Keeping my same routine helps my day go better, it helps me keep a positive mindset.*

I finish my run and get ready for the day and then head to my office. It is my routine. It is quiet there, too. I've been told that the office used to be filled with people hustling and bustling about before COVID. That's not the case now as many have chosen to work from home. And those of us that are working in the office, are wearing masks all day.

When I get to my office, I have no distractions. I dive head first into my training plan. It's my routine. I look at my training plan and I see my list of things to do to grow my business. I check them off one by one. I do the same thing the next day and then the next one and by the end of the week, I have reached my weekly goals. I celebrate, I crossed a finish line.

When life throws you lemons, you make lemon-aid. When life throws you a pandemic, you build a lemon-aid stand. There is no such thing as a "normal" day when you are an entrepreneur. Routine produces productivity even when life produces chaos. Routine offers comfort, even when you feel uncomfortable.

*It's been a quiet marathon, not the normal race where bands and people line the streets. It has been a difficult one to complete. I can see the balloon arch that lets me know I'm heading in the right direction. I look at my watch, although I already know I am not going to reach my goal. I keep going, I do not stop. I cross the line and I smile knowing this was my last marathon to ever run.*

My goal of qualifying for Boston one last time didn't happen. I was disappointed, but felt at peace. I knew I hadn't trained as much as I should have to run this race. I hadn't followed a training plan for this marathon and it showed. This was the last marathon that I would ever run, and I was okay with that.

# Chapter 10
# Knowing your Why

*I checked the forecast for tomorrow several times. Chilly in the morning, warming by the afternoon. I tried on at least 3 different clothing combinations before deciding what I should wear while running for 4 hours. My diet has been a healthy one these past few days and I have hydrated well. I need to go to bed early and hope for a restful sleep. I am both excited and nervous as I drift off to sleep thinking about the race I will be running in the morning.*

Being in business is much like the pre-race preparation. The end of each day should be a preparation for the start of the next one. What have I done well today? How can I improve tomorrow? I find if I end the day looking at the positive instead of thinking about the negative, I sleep much better. I almost always go to bed early and wake early. I usually get a full 8 hours of sleep. The nights that I don't sleep well are usually because I have ended the day with a problem unsolved.

A driven entrepreneur starts each day with a commitment to being all that they can be. Being action oriented and having a great plan of action is part of the daily challenge. Continuing to work towards achieving your potential is what drives you towards business success. Each morning is an opportunity to do better than the day before. It is a fresh start and should be seen as such.

As an entrepreneur, the challenge of innovation that not only grows your business but is a path toward helping others is why you choose to "go it alone" rather than working for someone else. Learning and growing is exciting and challenging. No two days look the same. We would get bored if they did. There is organization to the disorganization that is a normal part of our business.

There are many reasons to own your own business. The potential for success is in your hands. The drive to succeed motivates and energizes you. When you wake each morning, you "hit the ground running" ready to take on what life throws your way. There will be many curveballs. Keeping an open mind will allow you to work through these moments.

This is not to say that each sunrise will be met with gusto to take on the day. It is a mindset. There will always be those days that you will want to stay in bed, pull up the covers and watch Netflix. Sometimes we need those days to unplug. Most days are filled with the excitement of solving problems. The feeling of accomplishment drives an entrepreneur. It is one of the many pieces of our daily motivation.

The romance of business ownership compliments the efforts it takes to be an owner. There are days I ask myself why I take on the stress of business ownership instead of working for someone else. Being able to fill a need that transforms the lives of others makes my efforts worthwhile. The opportunity to grow and learn while adapting to changes thrown ones' way is another reason. Making money to earn a living is certainly a great reason to consider being in business, too. When you own your own business, you control your own destiny.

If you love doing what you do, then it is not work. This sounds cliché. However, being purpose driven ignites a passion inside a business owner that is difficult for many to understand. It is even more difficult to describe if you have never lived the life of an entrepreneur.

The day before a race, I work on "getting my head in the game." I push out the negative thoughts and focus on the positive. Instead of asking the "what-if's" I focus on what can be. In business, I often use this same technique. When something isn't going the way I had hoped, I try hard to focus on how I can change the situation to work better. Being a problem solver is part of the thrill of being in business.

Of the chapters I have written in this book, I have struggled the most with writing this chapter. Finding the words to describe the energy and excitement of being in business is difficult. As an entrepreneur, my brain is always going. I am constantly thinking of ways to do things more efficiently. Trying to solve problems and connect dots for my customers or clients is never ending. It is a passion that drives me. There is a fire in my gut that never goes away. It never gets old.

Taking calculated risks adds to the fire and excitement. Knowing that I am going to do everything I can for a positive outcome drives my passion to succeed. Strategizing ways to offer better business practices motivates me. In my opinion, nothing else can replace the thrill of starting a business.

The best way to describe what it feels like owning a business is this: You are about to step on the world's fastest roller coaster with the steepest hills. Standing in line you start to second guess your decision while you build up the courage to keep moving forward. It is finally your turn, and you hesitantly step onto the ride. Your heart is beating out of your chest. You are so nervous that you may pass out, your courage builds as the roller coaster starts up the first hill.

It is the steepest hill on the ride and it seems to take forever to get to the top. Click, click, click, the train slowly goes. You have no idea what to expect going down the other side of this steep hill, but the thrill of the unknown excites you. You finally make it to the top, when suddenly the train bolts down the hill and you scream with excitement! You do not know when the next turn, twist or hill lies, but you are loving every minute of it. You do not want the ride to end. When it finally does, and you catch your breath, you hop back in line for another turn.

If you like the feel that one gets when riding a roller coaster, I feel certain you will like the excitement of being in business. Hang on tight, you are in for the ride of your life! Thank goodness for the safety bar. This is your lifeline. You will find that in business, there are many safety bars to which you will hold on tight.

*I wake up early. I am both anxious and excited. I spot the clothes that I laid out the night before and start to re-think my choice of attire. A distraction that I do not need; wear what I chose yesterday. My adrenaline is pumping as I sip my water to start hydrating before the race. I see my race number, and carefully pin it to my shirt. The race number shows me I am part of something bigger than myself. I am nervous but I know I can do this. I have trained well for the race. I pass a mirror as I am heading to the front door and pause and step back to it. Looking in the mirror I say to myself, "You've got this! No excuses!" The door slams behind me, as I head out to run another marathon.*

# Chapter 11
# Winning in Business

*My alarm goes off at 5.00am. I am 55 years old, and I am still running. I no longer race after having had a few hip surgeries, but I run 5 days a week. It is my routine and my day usually starts better when I start with exercise. My feet hit the ground running by 5:25am. It is dark outside but the stars are bright. I carry a flash-light to guide my way.*

COVID 19 brought a lot of darkness to our world. Our nation, our friends, our families became more divided than ever. Businesses have struggled and so have relationships. It has not been easy. No one could have ever seen this coming.

My own family struggled through the pandemic as we tried to navigate our way through something none of us had ever experienced, and hopefully never will again in our lifetime. Everyone was doing the best they could, the best they knew how to survive both physically and mentally. The past few years have been difficult for almost everyone I know. We are all still trying to claw our way out of the dark hole that this virus had us in.

There has been a lot of darkness, but I have witnessed so much light! To see a young couple light up when purchasing their first home, or to help someone new in our community find a house to place their "Home Sweet Home" welcome mat never gets old. I have learned a lot about the real estate market, contracts, financing, marketing and so many other aspects of being a REALTOR®. But none of what I have learned can compare to the joy that comes from watching someone receive the keys to their new home.

It is easy to look back at the past few years and to think of how difficult it has been. I believe that most of us can look back and find many bright moments to reflect on as well. There is no doubt that most small businesses struggled during this time, but innovative thinking and perseverance of business owners also lead to much success.

I look back at March of 2020 and how I almost "stopped in my tracks" when I questioned if I should continue to move forward in my business as a real estate agent. I nearly quit, before I ever started. I love being in this business, and love helping people navigate the business of real estate. I am grateful I pushed forward toward this goal and that I didn't give up.

The tools that I need for success have always been there, I only had to take the time to find them. When I'm running a marathon and know I have miles to go, I "get in my zone." My zone is where I tune out everything else that's going on around me and I tune into what I am doing and what I need to do. When I began my new career and was struggling to find my way, I went to my "zone." Here, I focused on what I wanted to do and how I could get there. When I am in my zone and can tune out the distractions around me and those within my own head, I can focus on the goal I'm trying to accomplish. Getting in "the zone" helped me find the tools that were missing to launch my career. It turned my "I can't" into an "I can."

The real estate market is once again shifting, as it will always continue to do. I can continue to do things the same way, or shift my way of doing business. Using the tools I have in place for success and adding to or tweaking them, will lead to continued success. The key is in taking action. A dear elderly friend once told me, "When you stop, you turn to mold." I refuse to get moldy.

When I find myself running alone in the dark streets early in the morning, it can be scary. I hear sounds that I probably wouldn't have even noticed if the sun was lighting my way. My senses are heightened and I am much more aware of what is happening around me. I am grateful for the flashlight that provides light that encourages me to continue running.

Sometimes being an entrepreneur can be much like those early morning runs. It can be scary and many times I don't know what's hiding around the corner. These are the times when I am grateful for my faith. My faith offers the light that guides my way. It is my faith that keeps me grounded, when my legs feel heavy and I cannot go any further. It is my faith that helps me to get back up when I stumble. I am grateful for the Light I have been shown throughout this journey of entrepreneurship. And I thank the Good Lord for the many blessings He has sent my way throughout this adventure.

There have been times, and will continue to be times, when it is easy to lose faith and to wonder if it's all been worth it. Sacrifice, determination, and resilience are all part of the journey of business ownership. There are many more times in business when I'm able to relish in the successes that I have had along the way. The personal satisfaction of being a business owner is something that makes the effort and dedication well worth it.

Being an entrepreneur is living the American dream. The Oxford English Dictionary defines the American dream as ***"the ideal that every citizen of the United States should have an equal opportunity to achieve success and prosperity through hard work, determination, and initiative."*** In my opinion, being an entrepreneur is the epitome of living this dream.

Hard work, determination and initiative is how a business survives and prospers. Your hard work is your sweat equity. Taking the initiative to start the business is key to being resilient.

Determination allows you to persevere. Each of us has an equal opportunity to achieve success. Individually we decide if we will accept this opportunity.

When finishing a marathon, I am physically exhausted but am mentally excited. The energy is contagious as the runners cross the finish line. I am always thrilled when I set a personal record for my best finish time in a marathon. With the invention of the timing chip, family and friends can track me as I run a race. They celebrate with me even though they are not there physically. They have been following my run virtually.

When my children were younger, they used to run to my car when I arrived home from running a marathon. They would hug me as I slowly stepped out of the car, allowing my aching legs time to move. "Did you win the race? Did you win the race?" they would ask. I would chuckle and respond, "I did not win the race, but I crossed the finish line and I achieved my goal." The smile on my face showed them that I was happy with my performance.

In business we are always working towards personal and business goals. We may not always be the best, but we can always win the race. When we set realistic goals and meet or exceed them, we *have* won the race. There may not be bands playing loudly when you cross that finish line, but you can jump up and down with excitement knowing you won.

Your real win in business success will always be when you run your business with integrity. With any business, doing what is right is always a win. When you put your client and customer's needs before your own, you have won the race.

One of my favorite verses comes from the Bible and sums this up pretty well in 2 Timothy 4:7:

*"I have fought the good fight, I have finished the race, I have kept the faith. Now there is in store for me the crown of righteousness, which the Lord, the righteous Judge, will award to me on that day."*

Imagine crossing that finish line and having these words spoken to you as you receive the crown of righteousness… "Well done good and faithful servant!" Visualize this as you "run" your business and all you do in life.

# Chapter 12
# Core Value

*I am at a race. This time I am a spectator. My husband and I are running all over the race course to cheer the runners as they go by. Our youngest daughter is racing. She is a senior in High School. It is the last race of her High School Season. We take a short cut to sprint to the finish line so we can cheer her on as she runs. With one last kick, she crosses the finish line. She catches her breath, then turns to find her friends. They hug, congratulate and encourage one another, knowing some will be happy with their finish times and others will not.*

Witnessing the interaction between the competitors inspires me. Some are faster than others and finish first. Others finish later in the race but are thrilled with their finish times. There are those that finish the race, wishing they had finished with a better time. No matter what place they finish, they congratulate and encourage one another. There are tears, smiles plenty of hugs.

My husband and I have raised seven children who are now successful adults. They are all in careers that they love and several have children of their own. They celebrate one another's accomplishments and offer encouragement when there are disappointments.

Encouragement and wisdom are shared to help one another through tough times. Cheers and celebration are shared to congratulate one another when they have accomplished something they have worked hard to accomplish. It is part of their core value to show concern and kindness. The same is true of those young runners I watched in the finish area. Their core values are what kept them at the finish line to cheer on the other runners as they finished the race.

In business, we must know our core values. We must always stay true to them. Integrity, honesty, kindness, and reliability are just a few that come to mind when I think of those I admire that have a successful business. The podcast show I have, *"Keeping it Real with Sharon,"* found on Apple and Spotify, I talk to many business people in our community. Each business owner has their own story to tell. The one common value I hear from every one of them, is integrity. Is it possible to be successful in business without running it with integrity?

This question circles back to, what does success mean to you? If success means to make millions of dollars at any cost, you may want to re-think your business model. Those that I have witnessed that are the happiest in life and business have strong core values and they stick to them. It is not the money that drives them, it is the desire to serve others.

What are your core values? Do you have them written somewhere? Do you keep those values at the center of all that you do? These values are what will guide you in your business decisions. If you stick to them, they will help you make better business decisions that will likely lead to business growth.

I look around at the people in my community that I admire the most. These are the people that are service minded and give back to the community. It is the people who see value in collaboration and offer opportunities to do so. The people I admire the most are those that have integrity in everything they do.

To fully understand your business core values, you must first understand the deep purpose of your business. Why do you want to be in the business you own? What motivates you to continue? Taking a deep dive into your business motivation is an important step towards success.

How do you know what your core values are? That is an important step in the process of business ownership and finding your purpose. Think of the people you want to emulate. What about them do you like? What is missing in you that could be added? What are the principles you follow that will give direction to your business?

In my years of business ownership, I have always had a strong sense of giving back to the community that supports me. This includes offering collections for different charitable causes as well as being involved in different organizations that help those in our own hometown. Giving back and being active in my community ties into my business plan and is part of my core value of being charitable.

Reliability is another one of my core values. When I am working with customers and clients, I want them to know that they can rely on me to service them and to support them through every transaction. It is important for them to know that I am on their side.

Understanding your personal core values should help you when working towards your personal goals. They should inspire you in your mission to be a better person and a better entrepreneur. A strong set of core values will be what guides your business. Go back to those values often, and be sure that your employees know and understand them.

Promoting a culture of health has always been important to me. I understand the connection between living healthy and a healthy business and how the two go hand in hand. If I am tired and without energy, I do not perform as well. Our personal health and business health are closely connected. Making time to exercise is part of my daily routine. Living healthy is one of my core values.

Compassion is another core value that I find important in a healthy business environment. How is it possible to properly service my customers and clients if I am not compassionate to their needs? Working with the customers offers its fair share of frustrations. Staying true to my core value of compassion helps me work through those difficult transactions.

For me personally, Faith is my number one core value. If I live each day with faith, the other core values should follow closely. Starting each morning with prayer and meditation is a great daily reminder of how I should live each day. It is also a great way for me to reset and think about how I can do today better than yesterday.

Staying true to our core values can be challenging. Once you know yours, write them down. Look at them each day. I regularly need to be reminded of my values. Life happens and it is easy to forget them when you are thrown a curve ball. Those that I admire and are close to share many of the same core values. These are the people I go to that help me reset when I am not staying true to myself.

Once you establish your core values, work on determining your mission, vision and goals in business and life. There are many workshops available to help guide you in this process. I like to re-visit this process the start of each year. Are my goals still the same? Do I need to tweak my mission? Has my vision changed? This is a great way to start each year and a good exercise of self and business examination.

Intentional: this was my word for 2022. Each year I choose a new word. I had a sign made as a reminder and hung it on my office wall. It encourages me to be intentional in all that I do. Being intentional helps to keep me grounded in many areas of business and life. Consider starting this practice at the start of each year. For me, it beats making a New Year Resolution which I am sure to break!

*Respect. The respect the runners have for one another is admirable. Not only are my daughter and her teammates celebrating one another, they are also congratulating runners from other teams. I wait anxiously for her to come out from the finish area so I can congratulate her on a race well run. It will be a few minutes.*

The respect competitors show one another should be the same respect that business owners show one another. We are all in this race together. As the late Zig Ziglar, motivational speaker and best-selling author, once said, *"You can have everything in life you want, if you will just help enough people get what they want."*

www.ingramcontent.com/pod-product-compliance
Ingram Content Group UK Ltd.
Pitfield, Milton Keynes, MK11 3LW, UK
UKHW062258290726
14090UKWH00017B/756